A Missal for Little Ones

Illustrations by

Joëlle d'Abbadie

Magnificat · Ignatius

Translated by Janet Chevrier

The English translation of The Roman Missal © 2010 International
Commission on English in the Liturgy Corporation. All rights reserved.

Under the direction of Romain Lizé, Vice President, Magnificat

Editor, Magnificat: Isabelle Galmiche
Editor, Ignatius: Vivian Dudro
Proofreader: Anne Dabb
Assistant to the Editor: Pascale van de Walle
Layout Designer: Elena Germain
Production: Thierry Dubus, Sabine Marioni

Original French edition: *La messe des petits*
© 1992 by Librairie Pierre Téqui, Paris
© 2015 by Magnificat, New York • Ignatius Press, San Francisco
Printed in May 2017 by Tien Wah Press, Malaysia
Job number MGN 17025-R2
All rights reserved.
ISBN Ignatius Press 978-1-62164-037-0 • ISBN Magnificat 978-1-941709-03-0

Contents

Introduction for parents

Everything in this book is kept very simple, within a child's grasp. The Mass is a mystery, the mystery of Jesus, who died on the cross, rose from the dead, and opened the way to heaven for us.

In the Mass, Jesus makes present for us the sacrifice of the cross. He comes among us to offer his Body and Blood as our nourishment.

This is the essence of the Mass, which a child enters into little by little. A child does not need a lot of explanations but rather opportunities to grow in acts of faith, hope, and charity.

Faith in Jesus, dead and risen.

Hope of heaven.

Love for God and for all men and women, our brothers and sisters.

Mass is about to begin

Before taking a seat,
everyone takes a little holy water
and makes the Sign of the Cross.

Facing the tabernacle,
I genuflect to Jesus.

Jesus, I love you and I adore you

One day, Jesus said:

"Let the little children come to me."

And, so, Jesus,
here I am.

We make the Sign of the Cross

"In the name of the Father,[1]
and of the Son,[2]
and of the Holy Spirit.[3]
Amen."[4]

1. On the forehead
2. On the chest
3. On the left shoulder
4. On the right shoulder

I confess to God

My God,
sometimes I do
what is wrong.
I ask for your forgiveness.
Have mercy on me.

Blessed Virgin Mary
and all the saints in heaven,
help me
not to sin again.

Glory to God

Like the angels at Christmas, we sing:

"Glory to God in the highest
and on earth peace
to people of good will."

God gave us his Son, Jesus,
to save us,
and his Holy Spirit
to rest in our hearts.

Bible Readings

Lord God,
your friends of old
and your Apostles
kept your word.

They tell us
what we must do
to love you,
to love our parents,
and to love everyone.

The Gospel

Jesus,
you came down to earth
to speak to us of heaven
and to teach us to follow you.

I want to know you.
I want always to listen to you.

With our right thumb, we trace a cross:
— on our forehead,
— on our lips,
— on our chest.

The Homily

Jesus,
the priest explains
the things you said and did.
He gives us advice.
He reminds us of what we must do
to be your friends.

I believe
in God,
the Father almighty,
maker of heaven
and earth.

I believe
in Jesus Christ,
who was born
of the Virgin Mary,
and who died
on the cross
for us.

I believe
in Jesus,
who rose again
from the dead
and ascended
into heaven.

I believe in the Holy Spirit,

the holy catholic Church,

the communion of saints,

the forgiveness of sins,

the resurrection

of our bodies,

and everlasting life.

Amen.

Preparation of the Offerings

Dear Lord,
the priest offers you
the bread and wine.

I give you
my heart,
and I offer you
every moment of my life.

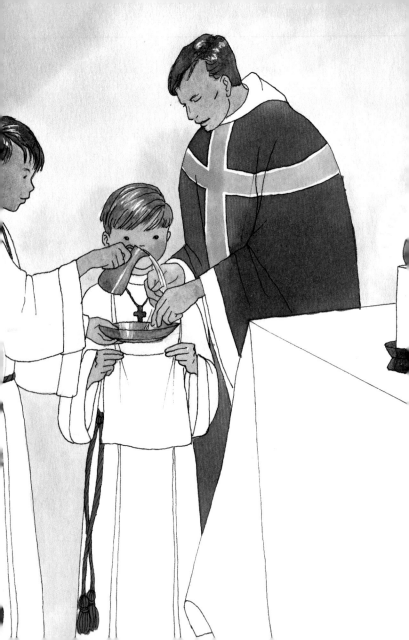

The priest rinses his hands

Jesus,
make my heart pure
and remove
all my sins.

The Holy, Holy, Holy

"Holy, Holy, Holy Lord
God of hosts.
Heaven and earth
are full of your glory.
Hosanna in the highest.
Blessed is he who comes
in the name of the Lord.
Hosanna in the highest."

The Consecration

The priest is going to renew
the sacrifice of Jesus.

We kneel.

The priest takes the bread. He says: **"This is my Body."**

It is no longer bread, it is the Body of Jesus.

The priest raises the host

and genuflects in adoration.

We adore Jesus, too.

Jesus, I believe,
I firmly believe,
that the host is
your Body.

We look upon the host
with love.

My Lord
and my God.

Then we bow our heads.

The priest takes the chalice. He says: **"This is my Blood."**

It is no longer wine, but Jesus.

The priest raises the chalice

and genuflects in adoration.

We adore Jesus, too.

*Jesus, I believe,
I firmly believe,
that it is your Blood
in the chalice.*

We look upon the chalice
with love.

*My Lord
and my God.*

Again we bow our heads.

The Mystery of Faith

Glory to you Jesus,
who died.
Glory to you Jesus,
who is alive.
Jesus, you are here!

Let us pray

Lord,
I pray for the Pope,
for our bishops and priests.
I pray for my daddy and mommy,
and for all my family.
I pray for those who are suffering,
and for those who have died.

May we one day
join you in heaven
with the Blessed Virgin Mary
and all the saints.

Through him, and with him, and in him...

To you, God, almighty Father,
with the Holy Spirit,
the priest offers Jesus
in his great sacrifice,

and me, I love you.

"Our Father,
who art in heaven,
hallowed be thy name;
thy kingdom come,
thy will be done
on earth as it is in heaven."

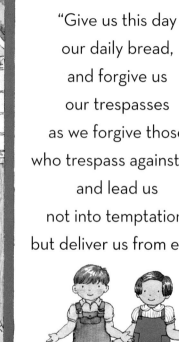

"Give us this day
our daily bread,
and forgive us
our trespasses
as we forgive those
who trespass against us;
and lead us
not into temptation,
but deliver us from evil."

Let us love one another

Jesus,
Lamb of God,
you who died
to take away our sins,
grant us peace.

Grant that
we may love one another
as you loved us.

Behold the Lamb of God

"Lord, I am not worthy
that you should enter under my roof,
but only say the word
and my soul shall be healed."

Jesus,
prepare my heart
that I may
receive you.

The priest gives Jesus to the faithful to feed their souls

Jesus, you are waiting for me,
and I am waiting for you.
You desire me,
and I desire you.
Come, Lord Jesus.

With Mary, our Heavenly Mother,
with my family,
and with everyone gathered here,
I keep silence and I pray.

I adore Jesus.

I thank him for giving himself.

I ask for his forgiveness
for the pain I have caused him,
and I ask for his help not to hurt him again.

I ask for everything good for me
and for others. I count on Jesus
to help me to love him
and to think of him often during the day.

The priest blesses us
making the Sign of the Cross

I leave
in the peace
and in the joy
of Jesus.

I LEARN TO PRAY

In the name of the Father,
and of the Son,
and of the Holy Spirit.
Amen.

Prayers for when I wake up

My God,
I love you with all my heart
and I offer you my day
to please you.

Virgin Mary,
bless me.

Good guardian angel,
watch over me.

Jesus, I thank you
for everything you have given me
this day.

I ask your forgiveness
for having saddened you.

Tomorrow,
I wish to love you even more.

Prayer to your guardian angel

Angel of God,
my guardian angel,
keep me
and protect me
throughout this day.
Help me
to avoid occasions
of displeasing God.
Help me every moment
to do what he expects of me.

Prayer to Mary

Hail Mary,
full of grace,
the Lord is with thee.
Blessed art thou
among women,
and blessed is the fruit of thy womb,
Jesus.

Holy Mary,
Mother of God,
pray for us sinners
now
and at the hour of our death.

Amen.

Ask the Blessed Virgin Mary to protect you always

My Queen, my Mother,
I offer myself entirely to you.
And to show my love to you,
I offer to you this day
my eyes, my ears,
my mouth, my heart,
my whole being.
And since I belong to you, good Mother,
keep me and guard me
as your own child.

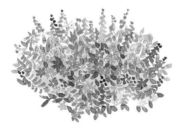

Lord, you know everything,
you know that I love you!

Jesus, Mary, and Joseph,
bless us, protect us, and
bless all those I love.

Guardian angel,
enlighten me,
keep me,
guide me.

O Mary, conceived without sin,
pray for us
who have recourse to thee!

Prayer taught by the Blessed Virgin
to Saint Catherine Labouré

My God, I believe, I adore,
I hope, and I love you.
I ask pardon
for those who do not believe,
do not adore, do not hope,
and do not love you.

Prayer of the angel in Fatima

Printed by Tien Wah Press, Malaysia
Printed on May 2017
Job number MGN17O25-R2
Printed in compliance with the Consumer Protection Safety Act, 2008.